Fantastic food

decorating

A WARM THANK YOU TO:

Oasi delle Primizie of Valente and De Cillis (piazzale Bacone 12, Milan, tel. +39 02 2049702) for the raw materials − *Pasticceria Cova* (via Montenapoleone 8, Milan, tel. +39 02 76005599): for the Sacher, page 27; the cakes with the sugar flowers, pages 22, 23;
and the buffet page106 − *Information Center for Swiss Cheese* in Milan: Emmental and Swiss Gruyere, page 88 − *Bellavista azienda agricola* (via Bellavista 5, Erbusco, Brescia): Franciacorta Cuvée brut − *Peter's Tea House* (Bolzano, tel. +39 0471 970506): tea and sugar sticks, page 26 − *Rigoni di Asiago* (Asiago, Vicenza, tel. +39 0424 63706): Butter mixtures, page 26; honey, page 29.
TOOLS: *Herbarium* (Padua, tel. +39 049 8968066): Hill Design terracotta molders for molding butter, pages 9, 26, 31 − *Pedrini PPL* (Concesio, Brescia, tel. +39 030 2185305): Tools of the Pedrini Più line, page 8 − *Beretta* (Milan, tel. +39 02 58304131): tools pages 8 and 9 − *Frabosk* (Lumezzane, Brescia, tel. +39 167 276760): steamer page 14.
TABLE: *Terra of Piazza Battista* (Pettenasco, Novara, tel. +39 0323 89666): chopping boards, page 30; plates, pages 52, 84; glass fruit bowl, page 41; centerpiece, page 100; glasses pages 32, 106 − *Geneviève Lethu Italia* (Milano, tel. +39 02313252) - *Porcellana bianca* (Arezzo, tel. +39 0575 320793): for the marble work tops − *Fiorirà un giardino* (Cussignacco, Udine, tel. +39 0432 602332): mats and plates, page 20; stone plates, pages 60, 64 − *Bormioli* (Fidenza, Parma, tel. +39 0524 5111): cake plate, page 26 − *Maino* (Milan, tel. +39 02 6686924): yellow and green set Philippe Desoulier, page 23; candlesticks La Rochere, page 67 − *Brognoli* (Gottolengo, Brescia, tel. +39 030 99512337): cutlery, pages 22, 23 − *Arte Fiorentina* (San Giorgio su Legnano, Milan, tel. +39 0331 411614): linen tablecloths, pages 22, 106 − *Orissa* (Milan, tel. +39 02 89402245): Indonesian and Indian plates, tables and wooden spice holder − *Joie de Vivre* (Cremona, tel. +39 0372 33620): baskets, pages 6, 7 − *Galleria Menotti* (Milan, tel. +39 02 29400447): candlestick, page 90; lantern, page 94; casket, page 43 − *Texinterni by Omnitex* (Milan, tel. +39 02 437942): fabrics, pages 40, 112 − *Zani&Zani* (Toscolano, Brescia, tel. +39 0365 644281): twine tablecloth for the photos, pages 48 to 84 − *I regali dell'Acanto* (Milan, tel. +039 02 2665394): colored glass bottle and glasses, page 36.

Library of Congress Cataloging-in-Publication Data Available

10   9   8   7   6   5   4   3   2   1

Published in 2001 by Sterling Publishing Co., Inc.
387 Park Avenue South, New York, NY 10016
First published in Italy under the title *Fantasia in tavola* by RCS Libri S.p.A.
via Mecenate, 91, 20138 Milan
© 1999 RCS Libri S.p.A., Milano
English Translation © 2001 by Sterling Publishing
Distributed in Canada by Sterling Publishing
c/o Canadian Manda Group, One Atlantic Avenue, Suite 105
Toronto, Ontario, M6K 3E7, Canada
Distributed in Great Britain and Europe by Cassell PLC
Wellington House, 125 Strand, London, WC2R 0BB, England
Distributed in Australia by Capricorn Link (Australia) Pty Ltd.
P.O. Box 704, Windsor, NSW 2756, Australia

Every effort has been made to ensure that all the information in this book is accurate. However, due to differing conditions, and individual skills, the publisher cannot be responsible for any injuries, losses, and other damages which may result from the use of the information in this book.

Fantastic food
decorating

Emanuela Caldirola and Sergio Barzetti

Sterling Publishing Co., Inc.
New York

Contents

Introduction

Can a simple potato turn into a rose?, a zucchini into a tulip?, or an apple into a graceful swan? Yes! It is not only possible, but is also fun and fashionable. There are ideas galore for bringing waves of novelties to our tables such as steamed potato flowers, fish-shaped lemons and grapefruits swimming at the bottom of water pitchers, spiraling zucchini garlands adorning serving dishes, carrot snowdrops, and butter bear cubs covered in honey. Garnishes can decorate appetizers, first and second courses, and even side dishes, giving them a refined touch of elegance. Reinventing our table is not as difficult as it sounds. All you need are food decorators, sharp knives, and a wealth of chefs' tips. Fruit and vegetable garnishing is an art that knowledgeable chefs have so far jealously kept to themselves. This book, rich in detailed explanations, reveals all the secrets and small tips necessary for making decorations in a masterly fashion, thereby rendering each and every dish unique and special. But that is not all—this book also offers you new techniques for molding butter and for making butter mixtures, such as maître d'hôtel, garlic, herb, and mushroom.

The Refined Art of Garnishing

Tools

To turn turnips, pumpkins, and melons into flowers, baskets, and other delightful objects, it is best to select stainless steel tools, as these do not rust with time. The most commonplace tools, such as melon ball scoopers, vegetable peelers, citrus zesters, apple corers, cheese slicers, carving knives, cookie cutters, and sharp paring knives can be found easily in big department stores or in well-stocked kitchenware shops.

- A set of different-sized Deco knives ("V"-shaped on one side and "U"-shaped on the other) for carving flower decorations
- Mellon ball scoopers for scooping out different sized balls from fruit and vegetable pulp

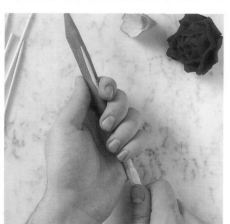

- Double-edged "V"-shaped and "U"-shaped decorators for making zigzagged cuts on cantaloupes and watermelons
- Scissors for finishing touches
- Pins (regular or with colored heads) for securing flowers, compositions, and making animal eyes
- Citrus knife and zester—the first furrows grooves into citrus fruits, cucumbers, and other vegetables, the second scrapes away the zest
- Vegetable peeler for finely peeling fruits and vegetables
- Apple corer for extracting the cores of fruits
- Cheese slicer for obtaining thin, even strips from potatoes, carrots, zucchinis, etc.
- Chef's knife for cutting the caps off watermelons, cantaloupes, and pumpkins
- Different-sized cookie cutters for making petals and geometrical shapes
- Tweezers for garnishing with gelatin and for arranging vegetable compositions on dishes
- Crinkle knife creates interesting ridged shapes
- Vegetable knife for making a wide variety of garnishes
- Serrated knife is ideal for use with pumpkins
- Sharp paring knife for trimming vegetables, carving petals, and giving finishing touches
- Spiral slicer for making spiral slices
- A terracotta mold for molding butter
- Different-sized wooden skewers

Main Techniques

Choosing Ripe Fruits and Vegetables

Carrots, potatoes, zucchinis, tomatoes, apples, watermelons, cantaloupes... the list of fruits and vegetables that you can garnish is endless. There are only a few "rules" to follow for picking out fresh produce:

1) Use fruits and vegetables that are in season—they are easier to work with and less expensive.

2) All of the produce must be ripe and completely free of blemishes.

3) The leaves, particularly of carrots, radishes, leeks, and spring onions, are the clue to the fruit's or vegetable's freshness and likely lifespan.

4) The fruit or vegetable should not give off a strong smell.

Pumpkins last for months as long as they are kept in a dry place in a basket full of hay or sawdust. Cantaloupes are easier to work with when they are still a little unripe. There are two types of watermelons that are suitable for garnishing: the dark-skinned ones, usually the first to be in season, and the round or oval-shaped green or green-striped ones, which usually come into season later.

Step-by-Step

Who is not surprised to see a potato rose or a tomato edelweiss for the first time? Anyone can perform this little trick of magic. Only a little bit of concentration and some creativity, which, with practice, will gradually become expertise, are all that is necessary to learn the art of garnishing. The step-by-step instructions for each garnish are described and illustrated down to the smallest detail. So there is no excuse for getting cold feet! When starting, it is best to tackle the simpler garnishes first, such as snowdrops, shamrocks, four-leafed clovers, mice, and bear cubs.

Some Handy Tips

- Always wash and dry the fruit and vegetables thoroughly.
- Do not wait until the last moment to prepare your garnishes. Flowers obtained from radishes, potatoes, carrots, and leeks will last for a couple of days when placed in water at 39° F (average refrigerator temperature). When necessary, we will give the ideal temperature for each fruit and vegetable. For example, very cold water spoils radishes but is indispensable for preserving leek and spring onion flowers.
- When using carrots, potatoes, zucchinis, and yellow and white turnips, it is important to use either demineralized water with 1 or 2% of pure 90-proof alcohol (used for liquors) or boiled water that has been allowed to cool.
- Once cut, a watermelon can be kept in the refrigerator for many hours. It is advisable, though, to wrap it carefully in several layers of damp paper towels or in a damp cloth. If you are planning to eat the watermelon, make sure the cloth was not starched or washed with strong detergents, as these could alter the taste.
- Cantaloupes that are cut in advance must be wrapped in several layers of damp paper towels and plastic wrap before being placed in the refrigerator.
- Once cut, eggplants, apples, and pears tend to go black. To prevent this from happening, squirt a little bit of lemon juice over them.

It is a shame to throw out any left over scraps; so, use vegetable scraps to make delicious vegetable soups and fruit scraps to make appetizing fruit salads, sherbets, and ice creams.

Steamed Vegetables

Potato and carrot flowers are beautiful to look at and tasty to eat. They can be served with meat or fish. A sharp paring knife is all that is needed to stop, once and for all, the dreary shape of steamed potatoes. It is easy to prepare this eye-catching side dish—all you have to do is follow the instructions for making roses, shamrocks, clovers, daisies, and sunflowers. It is advisable, however, to avoid making flowers with very thin petals such as daffodils or antique roses.

1) Prepare several potatoes and carrot flowers and then place them in cold water to prevent them from discoloring. Pour about 1 cup of water and 2 tablespoons of white vinegar into the steam pot and bring to a boil.

2) Line the tray with cabbage leaves and then place it in the pot.

3) Arrange the flowers on the tray. If the flowers are not all the same size, begin to cook the largest ones first and then add the smaller ones.

4) Cook the flowers for about twenty minutes. Remove from the steam pot and dress with extra virgin olive oil and parsley.

Individual Garnishes

Garnishing Tips

Carrot daisies resting on a plate of pasta, a cozy hen in a nest of rice, or a series of strutting penguins holding trays of little sandwiches are all perfect buffet ideas. Although it is customary to serve desserts and savory dishes together for a buffet, which allows you to place garnishes pretty much anywhere, etiquette requires that precise rules must be followed when it comes to traditional sit-down lunches and dinners.

Placement of Garnishes

Appetizers: The garnish must be placed on the left-hand side of the plate in the 9 o'clock position.

First Course: Flowers and leaves must always be placed in the middle of a dish (i.e. in the center of a nest of pasta or rice, or on the top of a timbale).

Second Course: The garnish must be placed on the top rim of the plate in the 12 o'clock position.

Dessert: The garnish should be on the top rim of the plate or at the center, according to the dessert being served. Desserts, however, deserve a chapter to themselves for explaining the techniques used in making suitable flower garnishes.

Gelatin

The art of coating elaborate vegetable compositions on a plate with a transparent film of gelatin dates back a long way. This technique was first used at important buffets and receptions to decorate hams, patés, and serving trays. Today it is used to decorate cold dishes, meat and fish appetizers, as well as many other delicacies. Numerous vegetables can be used for this garnish: zucchinis, carrots, peppers, and beets. Before coating the vegetables on the plate with gelatin, prepare them as below.

Gelatin

Follow the preparation instructions on the gelatin package. It is best to use soluble powdered gelatin. Once the gelatin is ready, pour it over the vegetable composition on the plates and trays. It is a very simple yet highly effective operation. For example, on Mother's Day, a zucchini and yellow pepper can be used to make a sprig of mimosa. On St. Valentine's Day the rim of a plate can be decorated with red beet hearts. To celebrate special anniversaries or birthdays, why not adorn the plate with colored inscriptions?

Zucchini

Wash a medium-sized, blemish-free zucchini. Scald it in a pot of boiling water and baking soda (1 tablespoon for every 4 cups of water). This simple tip helps to maintain the bright colors. Cook the vegetable on medium heat for 1½ minutes, drain, and immerse in a bowl of water and ice to halt cooking. Leave to cool and then drain. Dry and peel it with a vegetable peeler or cheese slicer. Place the skin, which will be used for the garnishes, on a damp cloth.

Carrots

Peel a large carrot with a vegetable peeler, wash, and dry. Slice the carrot again with the vegetable peeler or cheese slicer. Immerse the slices in salt water (1¼ cups of salt for every 4 cups of water). This will make them soft and easy to work with. Rinse them in cold water, drain, and place on a damp cloth.

Peppers

Wash a pepper, dry, and then shave very thin slices from its skin using a vegetable peeler. Immerse the slices in warm water for a couple of minutes, drain, and arrange on a wet cloth until you are ready to make the garnish.

Beets

Peel the beets with a sharp paring knife. Use a pair of latex gloves to avoid dirtying your hands. With a straight-edged knife, cut the beet into slices about ⅛" thick and then place them on a paper towel so that the juices can be absorbed and not stain your plates.

Grand Finale

Serving desserts is a refined art and those who love decorations have no other choice but to learn it. According to strict etiquette rules, garnishes must either be placed at the top of the plate or on top of the dessert, which is placed in the center of the plate. The positioning of the garnish therefore depends on the type of dessert. For example, if you are serving crêpes or a slice of cake, the garnishes should be arranged on the top-outer part of the plate. If, instead, you are serving mousse, ice cream, sponge tart, or pudding, the garnish goes on top of the dessert. Edible flowers are the most suitable to give a grand finale effect; they are even more special with a light sprinkling of granulated sugar.

Flower ribbons, or ribbons that are the same color as the flower garnishes, make stylish decorations for your dessert flatware.

Sugar Flowers

Every day nature presents us with flowers that are not only beautiful to look at, but are also good to eat. It is advisable to concentrate on the latter, especially if they are to come into contact with food. Some of the most attractive edible flowers are: orange blossoms, fleurs-de-lis, carnations, jasmines, geraniums, sunflowers, irises, lavender, lilies, mallows, daisies, forget-me-nots, peach blossoms, primroses, roses, dandelions, clovers, violets, and pansies.

1] Wash the flowers carefully and leave to dry. In a bowl, lightly beat with a fork an egg white and 1 teaspoon of water. Make sure the mixture does not become frothy. Dip a pastry brush into the mixture and spread it over every part of the flower.

2] Sprinkle the back of the flower with granulated sugar, and then turn it around carefully and sprinkle the front. If the sugar does not adhere to any part of the flower, brush some more egg white on it and sprinkle some more sugar. Place the crystallized flowers on a rack and leave to dry for several days in a dry, well-ventilated place. If your home tends to be humid, dry the flowers in the oven for ten minutes at 300° F. Crystallized flowers last for months if stored in an airtight container.

Molding Butter

Here is a new way to "spice" up jam, honey, salmon, meat, fish, anchovies, and cold meats. You can turn an ordinary butter stick into a bear cub covered in honey or maître d'hôtel butter into a garland of flowers. They can be served alongside lovely, tasty garnishes that are guaranteed to win over even the most demanding palates.

1) Place a mold in the freezer for about twenty minutes. In the meantime, take the butter from the refrigerator and let it soften to room temperature. Estimate about a 1/4 cup of butter for every mold. If you do not have much time, you can always soften the butter by heating it in a double boiler or in the microwave; make sure it does not melt. Once soft, press the butter into the frozen mold using a butter knife. Since the mold is cold, the butter will set immediately. Quickly fill the mold (2 or 3 spreads). Level the surface and then place the mold in the freezer for at least fifteen minutes. You can also mold aromatized butters and butter mixtures.

2) Remove the mold from the freezer. The butter should come out of the mold easily. If it does not, pry it slightly with the tip of a knife. Arrange the decorated butter on a plate and keep in the refrigerator until serving. Do not use margarine because it is too soft, which makes it difficult to mold.

Butter Mixtures

Maître d'hôtel Butter

This butter is ideal for broiled fish, thin slices of meat, and grilled meats.
Beat a $1/2$ cup of soft butter with a wooden spoon for one minute. Add a tablespoon of chopped parsley, a pinch of salt, a grind of pepper, and grated rind of half a lemon. Beat until well blended, and then press into the mold.

Dill Butter

This is an unfailing companion to smoked salmon.
Beat a $1/2$ cup of butter for one minute. Add two teaspoons of finely chopped dill and season with white pepper.

Mushroom Butter

Mushroom butter is perfect for canapés, croutons, and grilled meats.
There is a wide variety of mushrooms to choose from, such as honey mushrooms, morels, meadow mushrooms, and porcini mushrooms. Clean a $1/4$ cup of mushrooms, slice, and cook them in a slice of butter. Season with salt and pepper, and chop finely. Leave to cool. Add a $1/2$ cup of soft butter. Beat until well blended. Grease the mold with oil and then line it with plastic wrap. Use a pastry brush to make the plastic wrap adhere to the mold. Press the butter into the mold and refrigerate for twenty minutes to set.

Mustard Butter

This butter is ideal for lovers of strong flavors. It is great for canapés.
Add a pinch of salt and 1 teaspoon of mustard to a $1/2$ cup of butter. Beat the mixture, then press it into the mold. Use English mustard for a stronger taste.

Garlic Butter

Spread on homemade toasted bread, garlic butter gives that extra flavor to various kinds of cold meats.

Scald five cloves of garlic in boiling water for one minute. Drain, and then dry on a paper towel. Peel and crush them. Add the mixture to a $1/2$ cup of softened butter. Lovers of strong flavors can increase the number of garlic cloves or add a chili pepper.

Basil Butter

This butter is a wonderful accompaniment for fish and shellfish.

Beat a $1/2$ cup of softened butter and 2 heaping tablespoons of cleaned, finely chopped basil. Season the butter with salt, pepper, and two small grated lemon rinds.

Herb Butter

Herb butter goes well with broiled fish, grilled meats, canapés, and cold meats.

Finely chop some basil leaves, a small bunch of parsley, and a sprig of marjoram. Add the mixture to the softened butter. Beat until well blended and mold.

Honey Butter

You can use honey butter to sweeten up breakfast or an afternoon snack.

Make butter garnishes and then cover them in honey or jam. Use a flat pastry brush to spread the honey evenly.

Lemon Fantasia

Whether used to enliven your tea or to accompany appetizers and second courses, these decorated lemons are perfect for any occasion.

Lemon Bows

1) Slice off both ends of the lemon and cut in half. Holding one half in your hand, peel three-quarters of its length. Tie the curled rind into an amusing bow. Do the same with the other half of the lemon.

Lemon Crescents

1) Cut a lemon in half lengthwise. Cut the two halves into many slices.
2) Take a slice and, starting from one end, run your knife below the rind to three-quarters of its length. Roll the rind underneath itself. Prepare the remaining slices in the same manner.

Sailing Boats

1) Slice off both ends of the lemon. Cut the lemon in half. Cut a tiny crescent shape on the juicy part of the lemon, making sure not to detach it completely from the fruit.
2) Rotate the fruit 180° and cut a second crescent shape.
3) Lift the two crescent shapes and cross them over each other.

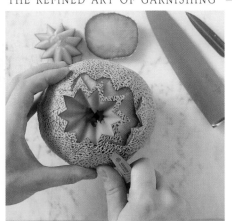

Ethnic Vase

All you need are a few well-cut incisions to turn a simple cantaloupe into an unusual bowl, vase, or original centerpiece.

1) With a chef's knife, level the base of the melon so that it stands upright.

2) With a medium-size "V"-shaped Deco knife, make various cuts into the top part of the cantaloupe so that you create a cavity. With a sharp paring knife, make a series of cuts following the zigzagged profile of the cavity—this will highlight the pattern.

3) With the paring knife, carve flowers on the melon rind to give it a sense of movement.

4) Make the petal's veins and remove the excess skin around the flowers in order to highlight them. Complete the vase by decorating it as desired.

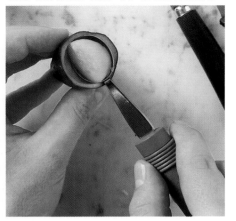

Tumblers and Baskets

Cucumber Tumblers

A quick aperitif, a relaxing "one for the road", cucumber tumblers do not alter the taste of liquors and are easy to cut, which make them an unique way to serve drinks.

1) Choose similar sized cucumbers. Cut them to the size of small tumblers, peel, and scoop out their pulp.

2) To make the handles, make a small incision on one side of the tumbler with a knife. Insert a cleaned slice of carrot into the slit, and then pin it to the cucumber.

Citrus Fruit Baskets

Oranges, lemons, and grapefruits make lovely baskets for holding fruit salads, ice creams, and fish appetizers.

1) Cut off a crescent shape from the rind of the fruit so that it will be balanced. For the handles, make two deep, parallel cuts in the middle of the fruit.

2) Make zigzagged cuts along the circumference of the fruit. Cut to the core of the fruit without touching the bases of the handles—the two caps will come off. Using a sharp paring knife and a melon ball scooper, remove the pulp from under the handle and from the inside the basket.

Ice Flowers

Bowls made of ice and flowers make original containers for fruit salads, ice cubes, ice creams, and liquors. A piece of advice—make sure that the flowers and leaves you intend to use have been cleaned thoroughly in case they should come into direct contact with food.

Flowered Ice Bowls

1) Pour some cold water into a large bowl and place it in the freezer. Once the ice has formed, take the bowl from the freezer and place a smaller bowl inside it. Secure the two bowls together with adhesive tape. Pour in more cold water and add flowers. Place it in the freezer for several days.

2) Take the bowls from the freezer. Remove the adhesive tape and put the bowls under hot water to remove the ice bowl. It can be kept in the freezer until serving time. If resistant flowers such as roses and daisies are used, the bowl can last in the freezer for about two weeks.

Flowered Ice Cubes

Flowered ice cubes not only give a scintillating effect to a pitcher of water, but also add a touch of color and freshness to ice teas, lemonades, and fruit juices.

1) Pick small, fresh flowers such as jasmines, field daisies, wild roses, dandelions, and forget-me-nots.
2) Wash well and arrange them in ice cube trays. Fill the trays with water and place in the freezer.
3) When field flowers come into contact with cold temperatures, they tend to deteriorate quickly. It is, therefore, advisable to prepare them a couple of days beforehand.

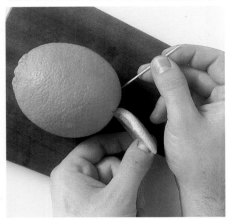

Goldfish

To serve water in a unique manner at a buffet is not always easy. An amusing way of quenching your guests' thirst is to place several citrus fruits, cut to look like goldfish, in a large glass or crystal bowl filled with mineral water. Oranges, limes, lemons, and kumquats not only add an original touch to the buffet, but also give a pleasant flavor to the water.

1) Wash the citrus fruits in water and baking soda. Leave to soak for one hour and then dry well. Cut off a slice from their "stomach" so that they lie firmly on the cutting board. Using a curved paring knife, fringe a slice in the shape of a tail. Secure it with a toothpick to the opposite end of the stalk.

2) To make the fish's mouth, carefully cut out a cone-shaped wedge from the stalk end with the tip of the knife

3) Use a pencil to draw the side fins and then cut them with the knife.

4) Form the eyes with a medium-sized "U"-shaped decorator. With the tip of the knife, cut out the fish's expression in the rind. If the fish does not float well, scoop out the pulp with a melon ball scooper. This will let it doze happily at the bottom of your bowl.

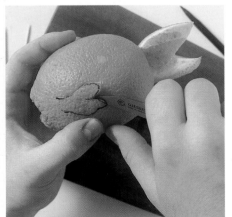

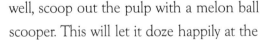

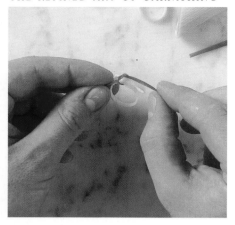

Rings and Bows

Are you organizing a romantic tête-à-tête, a dinner among friends, or a garden buffet? These garnishes are easy to make and are perfect for every occasion.

Leek Rings

1) Cut a clean, dried leek into 1/8" thick slices. Use your fingers to separate the slices into little rings. Open them delicately and tie them two-by-two with a bow made from a chive leaf.

Leek Bows

1) Scald the green leaves of a leek for one minute in boiling water and baking soda (1 teaspoon of baking soda for every 4 cups of water). Remove the pot from the heat, drain the leaves, and immerse them in cold water to cool. Drain carefully and arrange neatly on a cloth. Leave to dry. Cut out some thin strips (you will need two strips per bow). Gently bend one strip to make the first ring of the bow.

2) Complete the bow by gently bending the other strip. Secure the two tails together with a pin. Trim the ends with a pair of manicure scissors. To give the bow that extra touch, secure it with a pin to a thick zucchini slice.

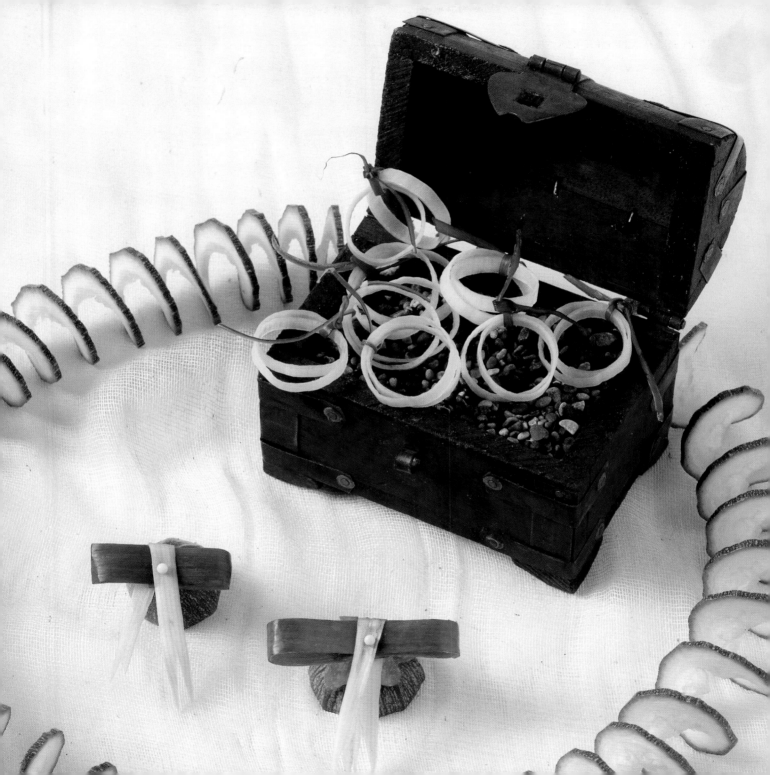

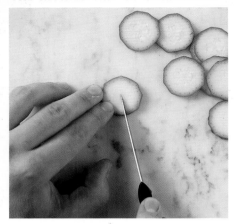

Spiraling Festoons

Round Slices

1) Wash and dry a zucchini. Cut it into even slices about ⅛" thick. Use a sharp paring knife to make a notch in each slice, cutting from the center to the outside.

2) Complete the decoration by gently inserting one slice into another at the notch. Do the same with the remaining slices.

Zucchini Slices

1) Wash and dry a zucchini and remove the stalk. Push the skewer into the center of the zucchini.

2) Gently rotate the blade clockwise until you get to the opposite end. Open up the vegetable carefully, making sure you do not break the spiral.

Flowers

Four-Leafed Clovers

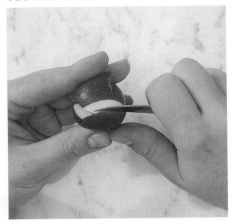

Radish Four-Leaved Clovers

1) With a sharp paring knife, cut deeply into the bottom part of a radish to make three petals. The cut flower should come off by itself.

2) Turn the radish upside down. Make three more deep incisions—this will create another flower. When placed in cold water, radish flowers will last for several days.

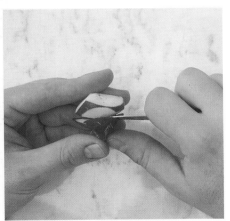

Carrot and Zucchini Four-Leaved Clovers

1) Wash a carrot and peel it with a vegetable peeler. Round off one end with a sharp paring knife.

2) According to whether you want to make a three or four-leafed clover, cut three or four petals with a semi-rotary movement of the knife. For the flower to come off, the tip of your knife must cut through to the core of the carrot.

3) Repeat these simple steps to obtain many other flowers from the same carrot. Just remember to round off one end each time.

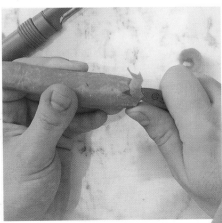

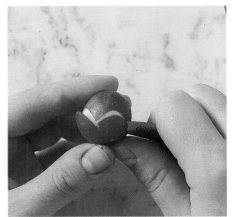

Buttercups

Buttercups are perfect for giving a colorful touch to salads.

1) With the tip of a sharp paring knife, trim off the root and make five curved cuts for the petals.

2) Use the first row as your reference point and cut another row of five petals. This will give not only greater movement to the flower, but will also prevent you from making mistakes. The rows of petals must be staggered, never parallel.

3) Complete the flower with one or more rows of curved cuts (the number of rows depends on the size of the radish). Immerse the flower in cold water so that it opens completely. If kept in the refrigerator, these flowers will last for several days.

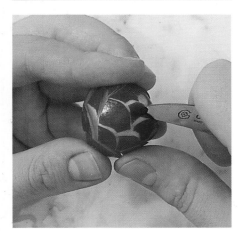

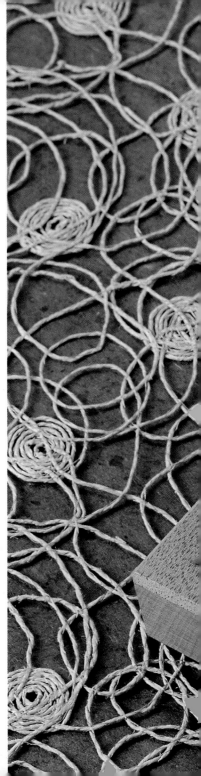

Cedars of Lebanon

Used for garnishing salads, trays of cold meats, and other dishes, these flowers are easy to make and at the same time are a very effective garnish. Bear in mind that the sharper the paring knife is, the easier and more precise your work will be.

1) Hold the radish between your thumb and index finger. With a sharp paring knife, make a superficial curved cut for a petal. For a good result, semi-rotate the knife.

2) Remove a slice about $1/16$" thick from over the petal. Exactly above this, make another petal and remove the slice of pulp. Repeat these two steps until you get to the top of the radish.

3) Follow the instructions in point two to make another three rows of petals.

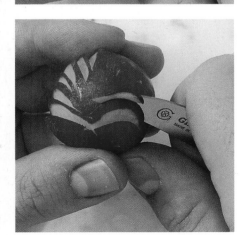

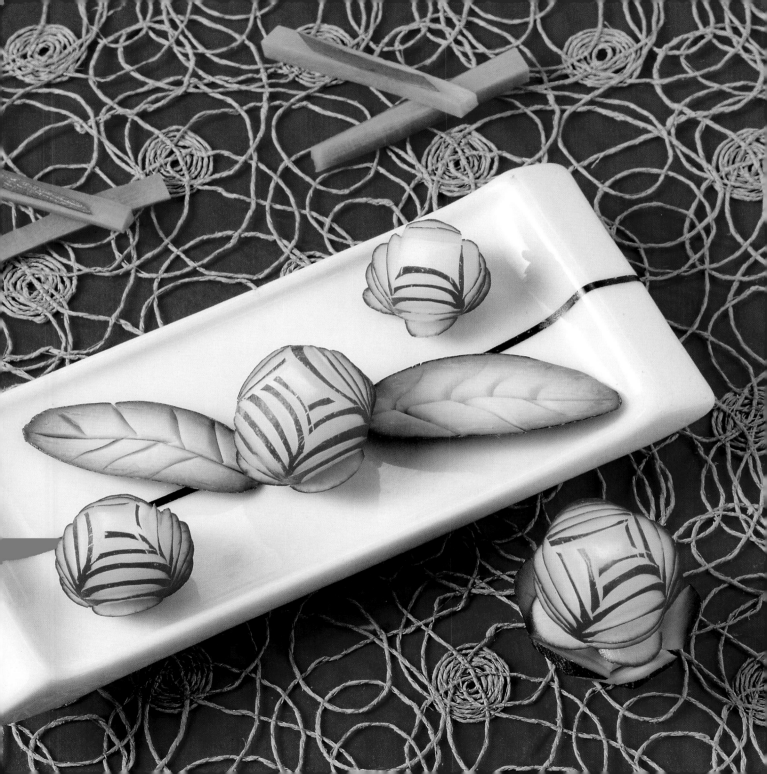

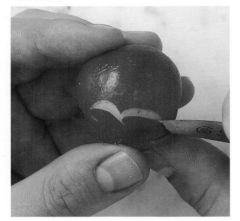

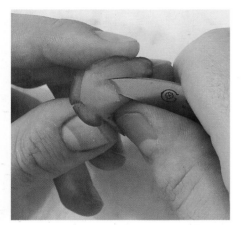

Daisies and Marguerites

Use a sharp paring knife to carve radishes and zucchinis into daises, and a melon ball scooper to scoop potatoes, carrots, turnips, pumpkins, and zucchinis into marguerites.

Daisies

1) Wash and dry a round radish. Take off the outer leaves. With the tip of a sharp paring knife, make a corolla of five to seven petals, according to the size of the radish.

2) With the knife, remove the pulp to shape the central part of the daisy.

Marguerites

1) Choose a medium-sized zucchini (there are more seeds in larger-sized zucchinis). Trim off both ends, wash thoroughly, dry, and cut into slices about 3/4" thick.

2) To make the eye of the daisy, insert the tip of a medium-sized decorator into the center of each slice and rotate. Then, with the smallest "U"-shaped decorator, carve eight to twelve tiny petals around the eye of the zucchini.

3) With the same decorator that you used in point two, cut deeply around the petal corolla making sure to reach the core of the zucchini. Lastly, with the aid of a sharp paring knife, remove the underlying excess pulp until the marguerite can be extracted.

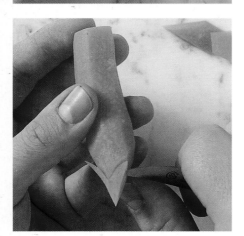

Snowdrops

All you need is a carrot to give a hint of color to any dish. In fact, it is possible to obtain about ten flowers from a single vegetable. Alone or with other flowers, also made from carrots or radishes, snowdrops are not only decorative, but also edible. Have them sprouting up in salads, rice, and all those dishes which require that crunchy taste and touch of color that only carrots can give.

1) Wash the carrot and peel with a vegetable peeler. Place the carrot on a cutting board, and, with four sharp cuts, make a pointed tip as even as possible.

2) Holding the carrot as shown in the bottom picture, make four petal cuts near the pointed end of the carrot with a sharp paring knife. With the fourth cut the flower should come off by itself. Every time you make a snowdrop, remember to sharpen the carrot into a pointed tip for the next one.

Magnolias

1) Trim off the root of a radish with a sharp paring knife and then make five curved cuts to look like petals.

2) Carefully insert the tip of your knife over the petal and, rotating it the way you would when peeling an apple, remove the pulp with one complete turn. The secret to a successful cut is to hold the tip of the knife facing outwards. Make sure you do not spoil the petals.

3) Make other petals above the previous ones.

4) Remove the pulp as indicated in point two. Repeat the operation until the entire radish has been cut.

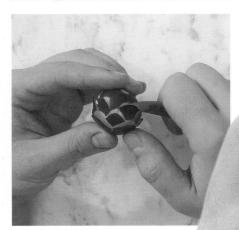

Chrysanthemums

Radish Chrysanthemums

1) With a small "V"-shaped decorator, start cutting the radish lengthwise from top to bottom.

2) Make as many rows of petals as the size of the radish allows, following a spiral pattern. Place the flower in cold water so that it opens completely. If kept in water, radish chrysanthemums will last for several days.

Leek Chrysanthemums

1) Trim off the roots from the base of the leek. Cut the heart 2½" in length. Make many long slits with a sharp paring knife. The slits must be parallel and quite close to one another; they must be at least ⅛" from the base, which must remain intact.

2) Turn the leek 90° and repeat the operation. For the flower to open, besides immersing it in cold water, you can cut a cone-shaped wedge under the base of the leek. Within an hour the flower will bloom.

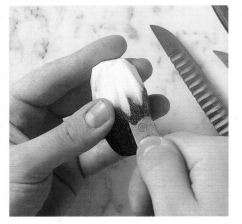

Tulips

Classical Tulips

1) Trim both ends of a medium-sized zucchini. Wash, dry, and cut into pieces about 2" long. Round off the ends with a sharp paring knife. To give the base a slightly zigzagged cut, hold the rounded end of the zucchini upwards, insert the tip of the knife, and, with the wavy movement similar to that used for carving petals, remove small amounts of pulp.

2) On the white surface of the zucchini carve five petals, making sure the tip of your knife reaches the core of the vegetable. With the last cut, the tulip should come off by itself.

Star-shaped Tulips

1) Wash and dry a zucchini. Cut it into pieces about 2" long, and round the ends with a sharp knife. Hold the zucchini with the rounded part facing your wrist. With a medium—large "V"-shaped decorator, start carving the petals from the top and move downward.

2) Complete the row of petals by inserting the tip of your knife as far as the core of the zucchini and then cut. With the last cut, the flower should come off by itself.

Bluebells

1) Wash and dry a medium-sized zucchini that has a protruding node. From this end cut about a 2½" long piece. With a sharp paring knife, smooth the imperfections to create a play of colors. Thin the node so that it resembles the end of a rose stem.

2) With the knife make five to seven very thin petals. The cuts must be very accurate and not very deep, so as to give a sense of movement to the flower.

3) Very carefully, so as not to damage the petals, scoop out the excess pulp from the central part of the flower with the tip of the knife; it will then look like a bud.

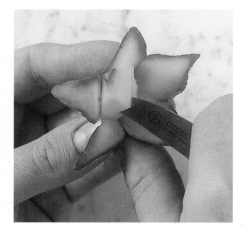

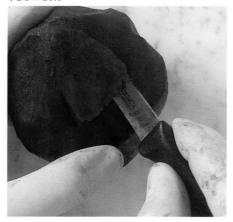

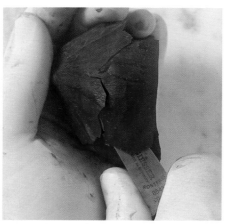

Carnations

Carnations can be made with white turnips, beets, zucchinis, and potatoes.

1) Wash and dry a beet. Peel with a knife and cut the root end into the shape of a cone. Holding the rounded end of the beet upwards, cut the base slightly zigzagged. Insert the tip of a sharp paring knife and, with a wavy movement that you used for carving petals, remove small portions of pulp. Wear latex gloves to avoid dirtying your hands.

2) Make five deep petal cuts on the zigzagged end of the beet.

3) Hold the beet in the palm of your hand and remove the pulp situated between two petals. Handle the knife with great care to prevent damaging the petals (the tip must be facing the core of the beet).

4) Repeat the instructions in points two and three until you reach the core of the vegetable.

Another Idea

To give a finishing touch to beet, potato, or turnip carnations, why not create a chalice with the nodes of zucchinis that you scrapped earlier when making spirals or other flowers? Here is what you do: with a sharp paring knife, thin the woody part of the node to make it look like the end of a carnation stem. For the flower to stand upright, carefully remove part of the inside pulp with a melon ball scooper.

Simple Dahlias

Beautiful flowers can be made with white turnips, pumpkins, zucchinis, beets, and potatoes.

1) Wash and dry a zucchini. Trim both ends. To obtain the eye of the flower, insert the tip of a medium-sized "U"-shaped decorator into the center of one end and rotate. Lightly mark the veins of the petals with a small "U"-shaped decorator. The cuts must be made from the outside and then inwards, towards the flower's eye.

2) With a large-sized "U"-shaped decorator, carve out the petals following the rays of the veins.

3) With the small "U"-shaped decorator, remove the pulp between the petals to create another ray of veins.

4) With the large "U"-shaped decorator, carve a second row of petals following the pattern traced earlier. Repeat the instructions in points two and three until you get to the base of the zucchini.

Pointed Dahlias

Even humble vegetables such as potatoes, zucchinis, pumpkins, beets, carrots, and white turnips can turn into refined flowers for decorating the table on special occasions.

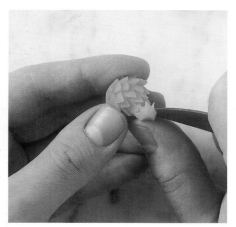

1) Wash, peel, and dry a carrot. On one end carve a row of tiny petals with a small "V"-sized decorator. Start from the top and work downwards. The cuts must be about 1/8" deep.
2) With the tip of a sharp paring knife, carefully remove a little bit of pulp from around the corolla that is facing the joint of the petals. This highlights the first row of petals and prepares the base for the second row.
3) Repeat the instructions in points one and two until you reach the tip of the carrot.

Antique Roses

The most beautiful antique roses can be obtained with beets, white turnips, potatoes, pumpkins, zucchinis, and carrots. Making a perfect rose takes time, but your patience will be rewarded. If you decide on making roses with potatoes, zucchinis, and white turnips, you can color them by gently rubbing them against a slice of raw beet or by immersing them in a solution of water and food coloring (doses are indicated on the packages).

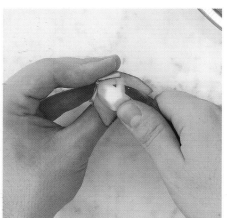

1) Wash and peel a zucchini. With a sharp paring knife, mold the node into the shape of a cone. Then make five finely curved petal cuts.

2) Run the tip of the knife under each petal to remove part of the pulp.

3) Make another five curved petal cuts and follow the instructions in point two for removing the pulp.

4) Repeat the steps until you have made incisions on the entire vegetable. To give greater depth to the flower bud, hold your knife blade, particularly during the last stages, almost completely horizontally.

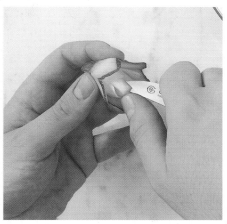

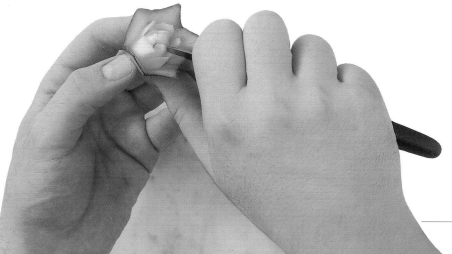

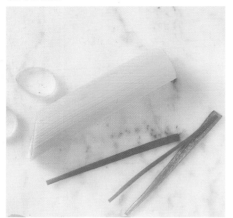

Water Lilies

Water lilies are very quick to prepare and lovely to look at, and they can be used to garnish salads or to give a touch of originality to leek-based dishes.

When cleaning the vegetables, remember to keep the hearts aside; they will later come in handy when making these garnishes.

1] Clean a leek and trim off its base. Insert the tip of a paring knife deep into the pulp of the heart (as far as the core of the leek), and make five deep "V"-shaped petals about $2^1/_2$" to 3".

2] Once you have made the last cut, separate the two halves and immerse the flower in icy water for several hours so that it can open up.

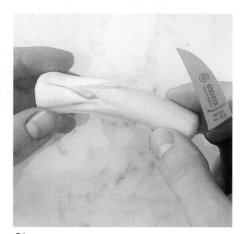

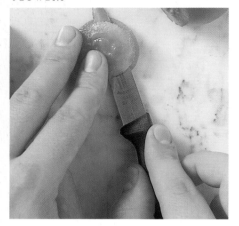

Tomato Roses

Rose Buds

1) Wash and leave to dry a firm, bright red tomato. With a sharp paring knife, cut off a round, fleshy slice. Place it on the chopping board and run the knife between the skin and the pulp to about three-quarters of its length. Open it like a book.

2) Use your fingers to separate the pulp from the skin. The bud is ready for use.

Little Roses

1) Select a firm, ripe tomato. Use a sharp paring knife to pare off a strip of tomato skin in a continuous spiral. Never start paring from the node.

2) Wrap the skin around itself to form a small rose.

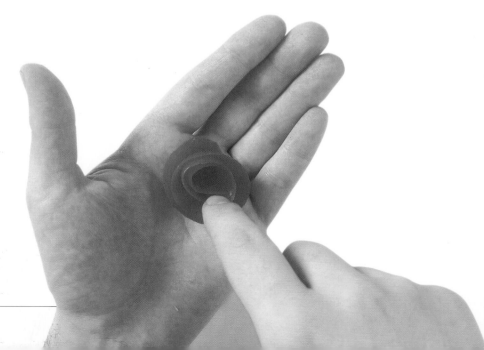

Poinsettias

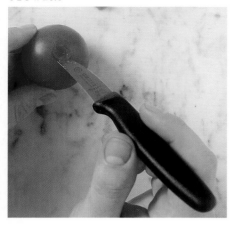

1) Wash and dry a firm, ripe tomato. Cut out a small cone-shaped wedge from the opposite end of the node. Insert the tip of the knife an inch away from the small hollow and follow its round shape—this will leave a thin strip of the tomato's skin around the wedge. The cut must be performed very carefully.

2) Carve five feather-shaped petals on the surface by holding the knife slightly tilted.

3) Insert the tip of the knife further in and contour the petal corolla with a series of cuts.

4) Sink the tip of the knife down to the core of the tomato and cut a round slice. In this way the pulp is removed and the flower can be extracted with ease.

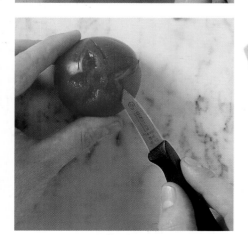

Roses

1) Wash and peel a medium-sized potato. With a knife, cut the base of the potato into a cone shape and make five round, thick petals.

2) Making a full twist as you would for peeling apples, run the tip of the knife under a petal to eliminate the pulp.

3) Carve another five petals and then repeat the step in point two.

4) Repeat the instructions in points one and two until the entire vegetable has been carved. If kept in cold water, these potato roses will last for several days.

Daffodils

These are ideal for decorating baskets and making elegant compositions. Daffodils require a good deal of manual skill and patience. Before starting work on the vegetables, make sure your knife is sharp. If you wish to create a more life-like effect, immerse the flowers in water and saffron. Potatoes, pumpkins, and white turnips are the most suitable vegetables for making this very delicate flower.

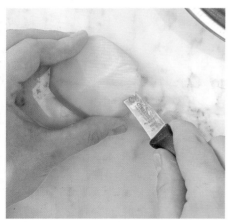

1) Wash and peel a medium sized potato and cut it into 2" wedges. Begin by creating four triangular, zigzagged cavities, which will act as the veins of the petals. To do this, divide the surface ideally into four equal parts. Insert the tip of the knife into each part and, with the same wavy movement used for cutting petals, remove small amounts of pulp.

2) Carve the four petals by making deeper cuts all around the vein pattern. Make sure that you do not reach the core of the potato with the tip of your knife.

3) Very carefully, in order to avoid breaking the petals, scoop out the excess pulp from the central part of the flower and then mold it into the shape of a bud. To give the finishing touches to the bud, use the same technique that is used to make roses.

Sunflowers

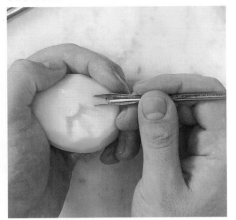

1) Wash and peel a rather large potato and cut it into wedges about 1" thick. Use a medium-sized "U"-shaped decorator to carve out the large central eye. To carve the petal veins, use a smaller "U"-shaped decorator. Cut from the outside and then inward.

2) Use a sharp paring knife to cut around the external part of the corolla. Use a movement similar to that for making pointed feathers.

3) Sink the tip of your knife just to the core of the potato and make a full turn to remove the pulp. The flower should come out easily.

4) Complete the sunflower by inserting a cluster of cloves into the center. Immerse the flower for at least two hours in water and saffron (a sachet for every 2 cups of water).

Mice

It's cheese time! And sprouting up between various types of Swiss cheeses are lovely little radish mice. Remember that cheese should be served at room temperature. Place the mice on the plates well in advance, and don't worry about them discoloring because once cut, radishes last for hours. If you prefer, prepare them the day before and keep in the refrigerator in water. Just before serving, stick in the cloves to make the eyes. Fondue can also be served with these amusing little animals.

1) Wash and dry an oval-shaped radish. Trim off the outer leaves but not the root; it will act as the mouse's tail. Level the base of the radish to make it stand upright. To make the snout, cut off two round even slices with a sharp paring knife; these will be the mouse's ears.

2) Place the mouse on the cutting board and, holding the knife perpendicular to it, make two deep slits to insert the ears (either red or white side up). To make the eyes, select two cloves of the same size and stick them into the face.

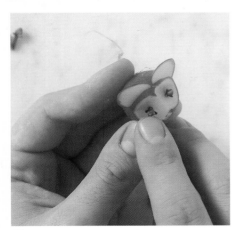

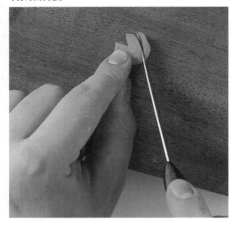

Birds

Let your imagination run wild and enliven your table with multicolored feathered birds. Kiwis and pears are perfect for this purpose.

1) With a sharp paring knife, carve out the beak from a slice of carrot

2) To create the bird's crest, use a frayed piece of a leek or pepper.

3) Take a kiwi, cut a small slit on the top, and insert the crest. For the eyes, pin two small, round pepper slices (you could also attach eggplant and zucchini slices). Then pin two cloves in them.

4) To make the wings, cut two "V"-shaped slits on either side. Then make another two or three parallel "V"-shaped cuts at about 1/4" from each other. Push in the cut pieces gently and they will slip over each other to form a wing. To prevent the fruit from blackening, sprinkle a little bit of lemon juice on the cut parts.

The Hen House

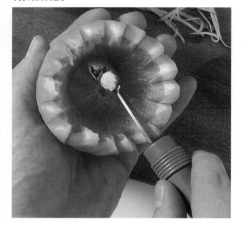

Hens

1) Immerse an egg into boiling water and cook for about eight to ten minutes. Remove from the heat and place them under cold water to stop cooking. To prevent the shell from cracking, pour a few drops of vinegar into the water. In the meantime, prepare the nest by scooping out half an orange with a large "V"-shaped decorator, and fill it with zucchini skin cut à la julienne.
2) Peel the egg and place it horizontally in the nest. Wash and peel a carrot. With a sharp paring knife, cut a thin slice lengthwise. From this, cut out two wings, a crest, a beak, and a tail. Delicately insert them into the egg. Use two cloves for the eyes.

Roosters

1) Immerse a large egg into boiling water and cook for eight to ten minutes. Place it under running water to cool. In the meantime, with a sharp paring knife, cut the crest and beak from a thin slice of carrot. Peel the egg and level the uneven end to make it stand upright. Secure the crest and beak into their respective places.
2) Cut out the wings and tail from a slice of yellow pepper, and secure them onto the egg. Zucchini and peppers cut à la julienne are perfect for making multicolored tails.

Chicks

Chicks are made the same way as the hens and roosters, but it is better to use quail eggs instead of chicken eggs.

Piglets

Piglets are quick to prepare, and are among the easiest animals to make. So easy, in fact, that children can make them too—in which case remember to replace the sharp knife with a plastic one.

1) Wash and dry a lemon. Level its base so that it stands upright. To make the mouth, cut out the node and rotate the tip of your knife to cut out a cone-shaped wedge.

2) With a felt-tip pen, draw the ears and then score them with a knife, making sure to leave them attached to the body. Stick in the eyes just beneath the ears—choose among cloves, junipers, or two green or red soybeans (according to the size of the lemon).

3) For the tail, cut the back of the piglet with a citrus zester. To make the curly tail, make a circular movement without removing your knife from the lemon.

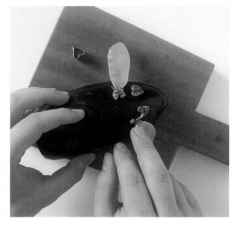

Sheep

Why not serve a salad arranged elegantly on a tray with a few field daisies scattered here and there and a grazing sheep? This amusing animal could also be used as an original place marker.

1) Wash and dry an eggplant and cut off the node. With an oval or heart-shaped cookie cutter, cut out eyes from the skin of a zucchini and pin them onto the pointed end of the eggplant. For the ears use two pea shells, but if you have difficulty in finding two of the same size and proportionate to the snout, trim them with a knife.

2) For the mouth, make a horizontal cut and insert two half semi-dry white beans or a garlic glove cut in half. These strange teeth will give the sheep an amusing look.

3) To create the white wooly fleece, attach many small cauliflower florets to the eggplant with pins.

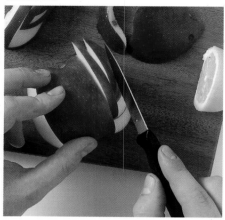

Swans

1) Wash and dry a medium-sized apple and cut off the node. Cut a slice from the base for the apple so that it will stand upright.

2) On the slice draw a swan's neck and carve it out with a knife. Sprinkle with lemon juice and set aside.

3) With a sharp paring knife, make two small "V"-shaped wedges on the top half of the apple for the wings. Finish off the wings with another five or six parallel, "V"-shaped wedges about 1/4" apart.

4) Push the wedges gently towards the back of the swan so that they are staggered and simulate wings. To prevent discoloration, sprinkle the whole apple with lemon juice. Lastly, fit the neck and head snugly in the node cavity with a pin.

Bears

Simply adorable and delightfully amusing, these bears cannot be absent at children's parties, buffets, or on the plates of young ones to encourage them to eat more fruit.

1) To make the ears, shave off two round slices from a kiwi. On the top of another kiwi, make two slits and insert the ears.
2) Secure two beans to a kiwi with pins to make the eyes. Insert a small carrot ball for the nose. Carve out the mouth with the tip of your knife.

Bears can also be made with pears—use the lumpy node as the snout and two cloves for the eyes.

Penguins

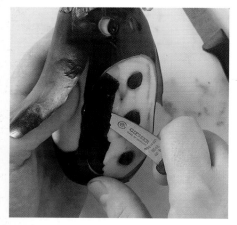

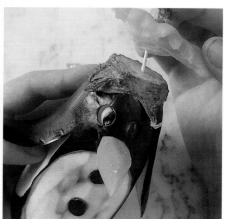

1) Wash and dry a medium-sized eggplant. Level the end opposite the node so that the vegetable will stand upright. Make the pupils by inserting a small "U"-shaped decorator into the top part of the eggplant and rotate it slightly. With the tip of your knife, outline the eyes and then, very carefully, remove a small crescent-shaped piece of skin.

2) To make the wings, use a straight-bladed knife. Make two cuts on either side of the eggplant in the shape of a pointed wing, starting from the bottom and then moving upward. With the tip of your knife, mark the penguin's stomach and then, with the help of an apple corer, outline the buttons of the tailcoat. Carefully remove the skin around the button outlines.

3) To make the beak, cut a piece of carrot into the shape of a cone, and cut it lengthwise to give a beak-like effect. Place it in a small slit between the eyes and stomach.

4) To make the feet, cut two slices from a yellow pepper into the shape of a raindrop and secure them to the body with two toothpicks.

5) You can use the node of the eggplant as a hat. If you want to add a personal touch to your penguin, slice off the top part of a red pepper and secure it to the penguin's head with a toothpick to make a sombrero.

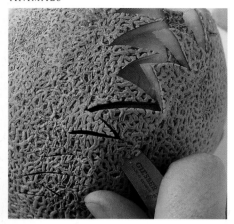

Cat

This cat is every bit as amusing as Puss in Boots in the famous fairy tale. Made from a cantaloupe, it is an original way of serving ham, port, and fruit salad.

1) Wash and dry a medium-sized cantaloupe. Cut off a slice with a chef's knife so that it stands upright. Draw the ears on the rind part of the slice with a pencil. Score them with the tip of a sharp paring knife.

2) Use a small oval or round cookie cutter to cut out the outlines of the eyes. Use a heart-shaped cookie cutter for the outline of the nose.

3) With the tip of your knife, groove out the pupils, nose, mouth, and whiskers. Make two deep slits in the top of the cantaloupe and place the ears in them. With a pencil, draw the cat's paws, tail, and some stripes (if desired), and highlight them by removing small amounts of rind around them with the knife.

4) With the same cutter used for making the shape of the eyes, cut out a piece of a yellow pepper (if you would like your cat to have yellow eyes) or a piece of zucchini skin (if you would rather your cat to have green eyes).

Watermelon Ivy

Decorated watermelons are elaborate garnishes to place on your buffet table, and are also a refined way to serve this summer fruit.

1] Wash and dry a firm, ripe watermelon. Level the base of the watermelon with a chef's knife on the node so that it stands upright. With the tip of a sharp paring knife, cut out a cone-shaped wedge from the opposite end. To highlight the cavity, make a border with a strip of green rind—to make this "border", insert the tip of your knife $1/16$" away from the small cavity and carefully cut around it.

2] Holding the knife slightly tilted, mark and cut out five feather-shaped petals on the surface of the watermelon.

3] Insert the tip of your knife at $1/16$" from one of the petals and cut deeply around the corolla. To make the second row of petals, cut out another five feather-shaped petals, staggering them with regards to the previous ones. This row of petals will be bigger than the last.

4] Repeat the instruction in point three until you have covered almost the entire watermelon.

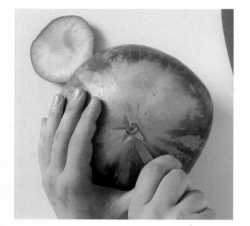

Pagoda

1) Wash and dry a round watermelon.
Level the base of the watermelon at the node
with a chef's knife. Roughly calculate the circumference
of the watermelon near the base, and then divide it
into six equal segments. Stick six skewers into the
center of every segment along the circumference.
With a pen, draw six fleurs-de-lis (the tip of the
petal must coincide with the skewer). With the tip
of the knife, cut 1/8" deep around the pattern.
2) Remove the rind around the engraved shapes
about halfway up the fruit. With a straight bladed knife,
cut out the first row of petals. Hold your knife semi-
vertically at an angle of 45° from your
worktop.

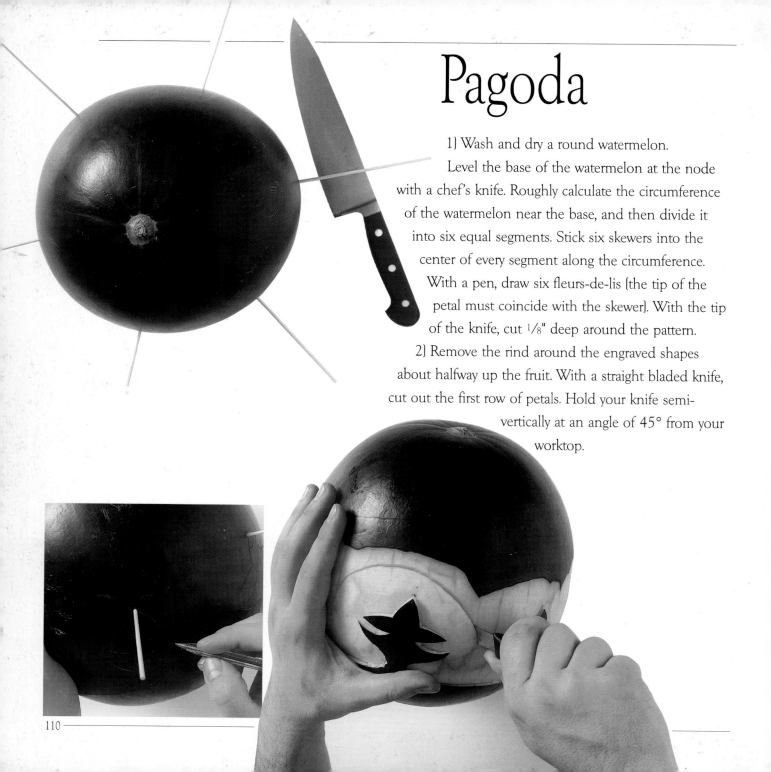

3] Remove the flesh situated between the half of one petal and the other by rotating the knife. By doing this, portions of rind will come off and you should be able to see the red flesh of the watermelon. This step is the basis for the following row of petals.

4] Holding the knife horizontally, make another series of petals and remove the pulp. To avoid making mistakes, follow the white part of the watermelon.

5] Repeat the instructions in points three and four until you reach the top part of the watermelon.

6] Using either decorators or a knife, decorate the top as wished with flowers, ivy leaves, or other fancy patterns.

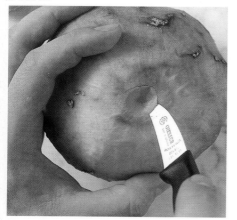

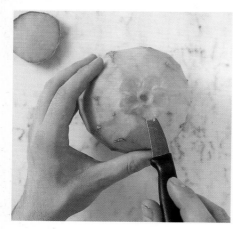

Dahlias

Cantaloupes carved in this manner can be used as decorations or as an interesting way of serving an all-time favorite summer dish—prosciutto and cantaloupe.

1) Wash and dry a cantaloupe. Peel it with a vegetable peeler. Level the base of the cantaloupe at the node with a chef's knife so that it stands upright. With the tip of a sharp paring knife, cut a cone-shaped wedge from the opposite end. Make a border outside this cone-shaped wedge with the green rind—to make this border, insert the tip of your knife 1/16" away from the small wedge and carefully cut around it.

2) Holding the knife slightly tilted, mark and cut out five round-shaped petals on the surface of the cantaloupe. To give the petals an uneven shape, do not make the cuts too cleanly.

3) Insert the tip of your knife at 1/16" from one of the petals, and cut deeply around the corolla. To make the second row of petals, cut out five petals, larger than the previous ones, between the half of one petal and the other.

4) Repeat the instruction in point three, gradually enlarging the petals until you have covered almost the entire cantaloupe.

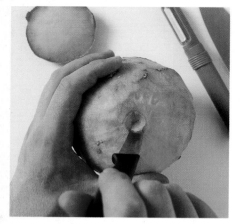

Buttercups

1) Wash and dry a medium-sized cantaloupe. Level the base of the cantaloupe with a chef's knife so that it stands upright. To create a play of colors, pare off the top part of the cantaloupe with a vegetable peeler. Insert the tip of a paring knife into the top cap and rotate it to extract a small cone-shaped wedge. This cavity will be the starting point for carving out the first petal. Use a spiraling motion to cut around three-quarters of the wedge until the upper half of the cantaloupe is carved.

2) Follow the petal outline with the tip of the knife. Small crescent-shaped pieces of pulp must be removed so that they highlight the actual petal. Make the petals following a spiral pattern. As you proceed, the petals will increase in size.

3) When the buttercup has been created, outline some leaves in the lower half with the tip of a knife and engrave some veins on them.

Decorated Pumpkins

Stenciling allows you to make beautiful drawings. When applied to pumpkin decorating, this technique creates excellent results for making lanterns, flowerpots, and soup bowls.

1) Select pumpkins with a smooth skin. If, as in our case, you are working with a rough skinned pumpkin, peel the skin with a vegetable peeler or a very sharp paring knife before stenciling. Secure the stencil to the pumpkin either with pins or with a little bit of spray glue and outline the patterns with the tip of the knife.

2) Remove the stencil and carve out the traced pattern with a sharp knife. The cuts must be about 1/8–1/4" deep.

These pumpkins can also be emptied and used as food containers.

Carved Pumpkins

By now you should have become somewhat familiar in this art, and should be able to perform several techniques simultaneously. If you know how to draw well, you can let your imagination run wild in decorating cantaloupes, watermelons, pumpkins, etc. with decorators and sharp knives. The pumpkin on the opposite page is only one example of this particularly refined decorative technique. Make zigzagged cuts with a sharp knife and remove the fruit's cap. With a spoon, scoop out the pulp. Draw your pattern freehand and carve it out with decorators and knives. Cloves and colored pins can also embellish the pumpkin (we used blue pins to give the effect of bubbles).

Index